MW00953269

Do not pray for ease of life. Pray to be a stronger man. Strong men aren't just born. They are made by the storms they walk through.

This Journal Belongs To:

To my four blessings from God,
Alexander, Matthew, Jacob and Louis
who have unknowingly inspired
me to strengthen my faith and given
me a greater understanding of what
challenges we all face in life. I'm a
better person because you exist.

A Message From

Throughout my life I have experienced great joy, great sadness, amazing positivity and deep bouts of negativity. I have struggled immensely through life's traumas whilst raising four young men on my own. Life has taught me many lessons and the most important one is, that no matter what's happening in our lives at any given moment we have an ever-present chance to alter our path by seeking refuge and counsel with God. As long as you have breath in your body, it is never too late to turn your life around.

I've learnt that when we seek salvation in the lord and hand over our burdens, regardless of how heavy they are, great things begin to happen. We can ask for forgiveness and look to the lord for help and guidance, knowing that our lives will begin to turn around and charter a much more favourable course, bringing much needed joy and optimism back into our lives. In these times, we need to prayer, reflect, seek forgiveness and ask for help whilst most importantly knowing with unwavering faith that our prayers are being and will be answered.

God has a plan for all of us and by turning to him, your path will be shown. I've gone through deaths, divorce and bankruptcy. I've been arrested, beaten, developed addictions and spent two years with crippling anxiety going in and out of court. In these times, I have known deep aching desperation and a huge loss of self and purpose whilst feeling my faith dramatically diminish.

Having struggled on my own trying desperately to claw my way out of the huge hole that I found myself in and looking everywhere for an answer and help, it wasn't until I began to turn to God that my life began to straighten out and joy once again was the main aspect of my every day life.

The Author

There is a wonderful transformation that will happen to you when you put your future in the hands of the miracle worker. All is never lost no matter how severe your current circumstance may be. New beginnings are on offer to everyone to free their mind and soul, regardless of our bodies being in captivity. You can expect to let go of a lot of pain, hand over struggle and be renewed by the work of God in our life's minds and hearts.

This Prayer Journal has been born through my own journey with struggle and salvation, from pleading with God for help to thanking him for all of my blessings. The harder my life became, the more I struggled internally and felt sorry for myself, but once I surrendered this way of being, the closer I grew to God and very quickly began to realize that he is always with us, walking by our side. From then on, my life began to evolve in a way I had never thought possible.

Being incarcerated is one of life's most daunting challenges, requiring an inner strength that has never been needed before. At a time where you may feel desperate, alone, lost and cut off from loved ones, you can begin to turn your life around this very moment by inviting God into your heart.

It is my heartfelt hope to you that by working your way through this Journal you will find much needed comfort, a new found sense of who you are and faith in your future.

Blessings to you.

Table of Contents

If we confess our sins, he is faithful and just and will forgive us our sins and purify us from all unrighteousness.

1 John 1:9

REFLECTION

We all have sinned and what a glorious God it is that forgives us and purifies us from our unrighteous behaviour. If you hold guilt, shame or sorrow in your heart, declare this to god below. Ask his forgiveness, he is always merciful and forgiving.

Love must be sincere. Hate what is evil; cling to what is good.
Roman 12:9

Lord, I am grateful for the following, thank you for...

Lord, I ask forgiveness for...

Lord, please guide me....

Personal Prayer Section

Dear God,

But those who hope in the Lord will renew their strength. They will soar on wings like eagles; they will run and not grow weary, they will walk and not be faint.

ISAIAH 40:31

REFLECTION

When your circumstances are bad it may seem difficult to fully trust in the Lord but this is exactly the time that you need to install all of your faith in the Lord. His promises are always good and true.
Can you remember a time that you have felt strengthened? Write about these times and how you can be strengthened now.

The **LORD** is my strength and my defence; he has become my salvation. He is my God, and I will praise him, my father's God, and I will exalt him
Exodus 15:2

Lord, I am grateful for the following, thank you for...

Lord, I ask forgiveness for...

Lord, please guide me....

Personal Prayer Section

Dear God,

When you pass through waters, I will be with you: and when you pass through the rivers, they will not sweep over you. When you walk through fire, you will not be burned; the flames will not set you ablaze.

ISAIAH 43:2

REFLECTION

Whatever you are going through right now, rest assured God is with you. He has been with you throughout all of your challenges in life. He never leaves you. How have you come through previous challenges? Can you recognize God's presence? Call on him now in the same way.

A friend loves at all times, and a brother is born for a time of adversity.
Proverbs 17:17

Lord, I am grateful for the following, thank you for...

Lord, I ask forgiveness for...

Lord, please guide me....

Personal Prayer Section

Dear God,

Do not be anxious about anything, but in every situation, by prayer and petition, with thanksgiving, present your requests to God. And the peace of God, which transcends all understanding, will guard your hearts and your minds in Christ Jesus.

Philippians 4:6-7

REFLECTION

Whatever we have done, no matter where we are, how deep our worries go, God wants to take these from us. Learn a new method of coping with anxiety by presenting your worries to God. Write these out to God below.

Humble yourselves, therefore, under God's mighty hand, that he may
lift you up in due time.
Cast all your anxiety on him because he cares for you.
1 Peter 5:6-7

Lord, I am grateful for the following, thank you for...

Lord, I ask forgiveness for...

Lord, please guide me....

Dear God,

Many are the plans in a person's heart, but it is the Lord's purpose that prevails.

Proverbs 19:21

REFLECTION

Time and time again we make plans only to find a detour along the way, ending up in a completely different situation than we envisaged. Maybe we need to pay attention to God with our plans for the future, he knows the plan laid out for you. Where you are right now may not be favourable but has it brought you closer to God? Note your thoughts on this below. What do you think God's plan is for you?

Your beginnings will seem humble, so prosperous will your future be.
Job 8:7

Lord, I am grateful for the following, thank you for...

Lord, I ask forgiveness for...

Lord, please guide me....

Personal Prayer Section

Dear God,

And without faith it is impossible to please God, because anyone who comes to him must believe that he exists and that he rewards those who earnestly seek him.

Hebrew 11:6

REFLECTION

Faith is needed to feel the rewards that God has to offer. We can struggle with this when we are unhappy with our current situation. True faith is having belief in the unseen, the yet to come. Look at the amazing world that we live in, all created by God. Use this knowledge to let your doubts fall away, tell him below why you have doubts and to help you overcome them.

And if we know that he hears us, whatever we ask, we know
that we have what we asked of him.
1 John 5:15

Lord, I am grateful for the following, thank you for...

Lord, I ask forgiveness for...

Lord, please guide me....

Personal Prayer Section

Dear God,

I am the LORD,
the God of all
mankind. Is
anything too hard
for me?

Jeremiah 32:27

REFLECTION

Knowing the miracles that God has performed can you see how he truly is the miracle worker? If he can create this world and all the magnificent glory that comes with it then he certainly can create a miracle that you can ask for to. Speak to God with true faith below, let him know your wildest dreams and know that he has listened and believe without a shadow of a doubt that they are on the way to you.

Jesus replied, "What is impossible with man is possible with God."
Luke 18:27

Lord, I am grateful for the following, thank you for...

Lord, I ask forgiveness for...

Lord, please guide me....

Personal Prayer Section

Dear God,

Because of the LORD'S great love we are not consumed, for his compassions never fail. They are new every morning; great is your faithfulness.
I say to myself, "The LORD is my portion; therefore I will wait for him.

Lamentations 3:22-24

REFLECTION

New beginnings happen every morning, bringing us a new day; a true gift from God. Having patience and knowing that our new path is unfolding is key to keeping our faith strong. Take each day as it comes knowing that you are walking aided by God himself. How does this feel? What small step can you take today on your new path?

You were taught, with regard to your former way of life, to put off your old self, which is being corrupted by its deceitful desires; to be made new in the attitude of your minds; and to put on the new self, created to be like God in true righteousness and holiness.
Ephesians 4:22-24

Lord, I am grateful for the following, thank you for...

Lord, I ask forgiveness for...

Lord, please guide me....

Personal Prayer Section

Dear God,

Every morning
and noon I cry
out in distress
and he hears my
voice

Psalm 55:17

REFLECTION

The more we prayer, the closer we become to God. Establishing a practice of praying several times per day will bring great rewards. This can be simple, quiet prayer spoken within your mind and heart or strong, emotional prayer read out loud, its your connection with God, your way. Write below how often you feel like you need to speak to God and why. Know that he hears you.

Whether you turn to the right or to the left, your ears will hear a voice
behind you, saying, "This is the way; walk in it.
Isaiah 30:21

Lord, I am grateful for the following, thank you for...

Lord, I ask forgiveness for...

Lord, please guide me....

Personal Prayer Section

Dear God,

Therefore do not worry about tomorrow, for tomorrow will worry about itself. Each day has enough trouble of its own.

Matthew 6:34

REFLECTION

As you strengthen your walk with God, start to learn to live in each moment, be in the now. One step at a time, each moment of each day see where you can find the joy. Do not spend today worrying about tomorrow, enjoy the moment as it is. Find happiness in the smallest of things. What does the present moment feel like to you? Can you find joy?

The Lord is merciful and forgiving.
Daniel 9:9

Lord, I am grateful for the following, thank you for...

Lord, I ask forgiveness for...

Lord, please guide me....

Dear God,

40

Trust in the Lord
with all your heart
and lean not on
your own
understanding.

Proverbs 3:5

REFLECTION

When it is hard to work out why we are where we are in our life right now, it is good to remember that God has plans for you and knows what is best for you. Teaching you a struggle so that you can lead others on their journey perhaps? What lessons are you learning that you may have needed to learn?

He is the one you praise; he is your God, who performed for you those great and awesome wonders you saw with your own eyes.
Deuteronomy 10:21

Lord, I am grateful for the following, thank you for...

Lord, I ask forgiveness for...

Lord, please guide me....

Personal Prayer Section

Dear God,

Very early in the morning, while it was still dark, Jesus got up, left the house and went off to a solitary place, where he prayed.

Mark 1:35

REFLECTION

Use the moments, the early hours, the middle of the nights, the quiet late afternoons to pray. The power of prayer is incredible. Use these moments, not to fret but to become stronger. Write below how and when you can do this and how you will benefit.

If you believe, you will receive whatever you ask for in prayer.
Matthew 21:22

Lord, I am grateful for the following, thank you for...

Lord, I ask forgiveness for...

Lord, please guide me....

Personal Prayer Section

Dear God,

No temptation has overtaken you except what is common to mankind. And God is faithful; he will not let you be tempted beyond what you can bear. But when you are tempted, he will also provide a way out so that you can endure it.

1 Corinthians 10:13

REFLECTION

What temptations do you struggle with? Whatever temptations you struggle
with, God will provide a way out for you.
We all feel tempted at times, seek God for his support when the urge is strong.

Can a man walk on hot coals
without his feet being scorched?
Proverbs 6:28

Lord, I am grateful for the following, thank you for...

Lord, I ask forgiveness for...

Lord, please guide me....

Personal Prayer Section

Dear God,

If my people, who are called by my name, will humble themselves and pray and seek my face and turn from their wicked ways, then I will hear from heaven and I will forgive their sin and will heal their land.

2 Chronicles 7:14

REFLECTION

No matter what the sin is, no matter what you have done, when you have lost your way, God will hear you, forgive you and provide much needed healing if you only turn to him and confess. A heartfelt confession with true admittance and humility. What is weighing heavy on you? Can you give this to God right now?

The righteous cry out, and the Lord hears them; he delivers them from
all their troubles.
Psalm 34:17

Lord, I am grateful for the following, thank you for...

Lord, I ask forgiveness for...

Lord, please guide me....

Personal Prayer Section

Dear God,

For we are God's handiwork, created in Christ Jesus to do good works, which God prepared in advance for us to do.

Ephesians 2:10

REFLECTION

We all have unique gifts, abilities and talents.
EVERY ONE OF US! No one is exempt.
Do you know your God given gift?
Do you know how to use them?
Can you use them to bless others?

And I will do whatever you ask in my name, so that the Father may be glorified in the Son.
John 14:13

Lord, I am grateful for the following, thank you for...

Lord, I ask forgiveness for...

Lord, please guide me....

Personal Prayer Section

Dear God,

If any of you lacks wisdom, you should ask God, who gives generously to all without finding fault, and it will be given to you.

James 1:5

REFLECTION

Sometimes we really don't have a clue what to do next. We have no experience, no knowledge to turn to and are completely lost. I know many times I have prayed, "Dear God, what am I to do now, I have no clue!" Ask God for Wisdom, ask to be enlightened, he knows what you need.

Then you will call on me and come and pray to me, and I will listen to you.
Jeremiah 29:12

Lord, I am grateful for the following, thank you for...

Lord, I ask forgiveness for...

Lord, please guide me....

Dear God,

Not only so, but we also glory in our sufferings, because we know that suffering produces perseverance; perseverance, character; and character, hope. And hope does not put us to shame because God's love has been poured out into our hearts through the Holy Spirit, who has been given to us.

Romans 5:3-5

REFLECTION

Have you every thought that life's sufferings maybe working for us and not too us? That within Christianity suffering is bringing us closer to God? Who did Jesus spend his time with? The poor, the outcasts, the criminals, that's who, to save them. This time in your life will change you. Write down how it can change you for the better.

Answer me when I call to you, my righteous God. Give me relief from my distress; have mercy on me and hear my prayer.
Psalm 4:1

Lord, I am grateful for the following, thank you for...

Lord, I ask forgiveness for...

Lord, please guide me....

Personal Prayer Section

Dear God,

Therefore confess your
sins to each other and
pray for each other so
that you may be
healed. The prayer of
a righteous person is
powerful and effective.

James 5:16

REFLECTION

There is so much freedom to be gained when you can be open and honest with others and God is stating here that to confess your sins to other Christians will produce a powerful healing for all.
Do you feel that you have other Christians to talk to in this way? How would you feel doing this?

And I will do whatever you ask in my name, so that the Father may be
glorified in the Son.
John 14:13

Lord, I am grateful for the following, thank you for...

Lord, I ask forgiveness for...

Lord, please guide me....

_____
_____
_____
_____
_____
_____
_____
_____
_____
_____
_____
_____
_____
_____
_____
_____

Personal Prayer Section

Dear God,

_____
_____
_____
_____
_____
_____
_____
_____
_____
_____
_____
_____
_____
_____
_____
_____
_____
_____

The Lord himself goes before you and will be with you; he will never leave you nor forsake you. Do not be afraid; do not be discouraged.

Deuteronomy 31:8

REFLECTION

Follow him and be with him throughout your journey in times of discouragement, disappointment and desperation. He is with you and you can seek refuge in him.

What do you need to hand over to him now to regain your courage and faith?

Be joyful in hope, patient in affliction, faithful in prayer.
Romans 12:12

Lord, I am grateful for the following, thank you for...

Lord, I ask forgiveness for...

Lord, please guide me....

Personal Prayer Section

Dear God,

Dear children, let us not love with words or speech but with actions and in truth.

1 John 3:18

REFLECTION

How many times do you do things for others without thinking about what is in it for you? Are you able to help others from a place of love without thinking of yourself? What do others do for you in this way and how can you also do this?

In the same way, the Spirit helps us in our weakness. We do not know what we ought to pray for, but the Spirit himself intercedes for us through wordless groans.
Romans 8:26

Lord, I am grateful for the following, thank you for...

Lord, I ask forgiveness for...

Lord, please guide me....

Personal Prayer Section

Dear God,

Even though I walk
through the darkest
valley,
I will fear no evil,
for you are with me;
your rod and your
staff, they comfort
me.

Psalm 23:4

REFLECTION

The right paths for us, our current paths can feel frightening at times, dark and unknown but with God as our companion we have nothing to fear.
Think of the darkest valley that you have had to walk through and how God's presence helped you through it. Can you call on that experience now?

The Lord hears the needy and does not despise his captive people.
PSALM 69:33

Lord, I am grateful for the following, thank you for...

Lord, I ask forgiveness for...

Lord, please guide me....

Personal Prayer Section

Dear God,

Then he adds:
"Their sins and
lawless acts I will
remember no
more."

Hebrews 10:17

REFLECTION

When you repent and confess your sins they belong to you no more. The Lord does not hold onto these and ask you to carry them for the rest of your life. You are free to start living in a different way without the weight of the past. How does it feel to have the burden of your sins lifted from you? What will you do differently in the future?

So watch yourselves. "If your brother or sister sins against you, rebuke them; and if they repent, forgive them.
Even if they sin against you seven times in a day and seven times come back to you saying 'I repent,' you must forgive them
Luke 17:3-4

Lord, I am grateful for the following, thank you for...

Lord, I ask forgiveness for...

Lord, please guide me....

Personal Prayer Section

Dear God,

May the God of hope
fill you with all joy
and peace in
believing, so that by
the power of the Holy
Spirit you may
abound in hope.

Romans 15:13

REFLECTION

When was the last time that you felt truly hopeful? That the future looked bright and all worries were gone? True belief in God answering your prayers provides you with the serenity of peace and hope. How does it feel to have hope of this magnitude?

Count it all joy, my brothers, when you meet trials of various kinds
James 1:2

Lord, I am grateful for the following, thank you for...

Lord, I ask forgiveness for...

Lord, please guide me....

Personal Prayer Section

Dear God,

Until now you
have asked
nothing in my
name. Ask, and
you will receive,
that your joy may
be full.

John 16:24

REFLECTION

Have you ever really prayed to God for yourself of what you would like
for you. What would really make you happy? Worries aside, dig deep
and state your top desires to God below.

A joyful heart is good medicine, but a crushed spirit dries up the bones
Proverbs 17:22

Lord, I am grateful for the following, thank you for...

Lord, I ask forgiveness for...

Lord, please guide me....

Personal Prayer Section

Dear God,

Let us not become weary in doing good, for at the proper time we will reap a harvest if we do not give up.

Galatians 6:9

REFLECTION

Reaping what we sow; well it's true isn't it? Think back on how your actions have produced the circumstances that you find yourself in now. Doing good may not seem to feel as if we are getting anywhere at first but rest assured you will be paid back ten fold. Such is the work of the Lord. In what ways are you doing good and how can you expand this to all areas of your life?

And God is able to bless you abundantly, so that in all things at all times,
having all that you need, you will abound in every good work
2 Corinthians 9:8

Lord, I am grateful for the following, thank you for...

Lord, I ask forgiveness for...

Lord, please guide me....

Personal Prayer Section

Dear God,

I am with you and will watch over you wherever you go, and I will bring you back to this land. I will not leave you until I have done what I have promised you

Genesis 28:15

REFLECTION

God is asking for your belief here, whilst travelling your road of transformation. It's all so easy to forget that you have a larger purpose to your life and live in fear, but you can find confidence and meaning in Gods words and promises to you. Do you find it hard to believe sometimes that you have a brighter purpose and plan? What signs/opportunities can you see before you?

Commit to the LORD whatever you do, and he will establish your plans.
Proverbs 16:3

Lord, I am grateful for the following, thank you for...

Lord, I ask forgiveness for...

Lord, please guide me....

Personal Prayer Section

Dear God,

Say to those with fearful hearts, "Be strong, do not fear; your God will come, he will come with vengeance; with divine retribution he will come to save you.

Isaiah 35:4

REFLECTION

God is here right now and is working to make things right. He promises restoration, repair, healing and transformation to all with fear in their hearts. What causes your heart to race, what causes you to feel helpless or doomed? Reflect on this now and hand the causes over to God.

Jesus looked at them and said, "With man this is impossible, but with God all things are possible
Matthew 19:26

Lord, I am grateful for the following, thank you for...

Lord, I ask forgiveness for...

Lord, please guide me....

Personal Prayer Section

Dear God,

Peace I leave with you; my peace I give you. I do not give to you as the world gives. Do not let your hearts be troubled and do not be afraid.

John 14:27

REFLECTION

The peace Christ offers here refers to a hope and reassurance that is not of this 'man world' but of the world offered by the eternal. It is a guaranteed peace that you can look to when the "not knowing" brings its own kind of terror. If you are suffering, you can acknowledge that here whilst at the same time trusting in God to come through on his promises.

The LORD is my light and my salvation— whom shall I fear? The
LORD is the stronghold of my life— of whom shall I be afraid?
Psalm 27:1

Lord, I am grateful for the following, thank you for...

Lord, I ask forgiveness for...

Lord, please guide me....

Dear God,

Have I not commanded you? Be strong and courageous. Do not be afraid; do not be discouraged, for the LORD your God will be with you wherever you go.

Joshua 1:9

REFLECTION

One of the most powerful verses in the bible that can speak to almost every challenge that we face in life. You can apply this to your life knowing that you can be strong and courageous and sure that God will be with you, when you pursue his mission, obey his word and remain steadfast in your calling. Do you actively pursue God's mission? How can you do this?

When hard pressed, I cried to the LORD; he brought me into a spacious place. The LORD is with me; I will not be afraid. What can mere mortals do to me?
Psalm 118:5-6

Lord, I am grateful for the following, thank you for...

Lord, I ask forgiveness for...

Lord, please guide me....

Personal Prayer Section

Dear God,

Let us then approach God's throne of grace with confidence, so that we may receive mercy and find grace to help us in our time of need.

Hebrews 4:16

REFLECTION

Nothing is hidden from God who is our ultimate judge and his word is the measuring stick for all of our thoughts, deeds and intentions. We all experience suffering, temptation and failures but they are fully understood by Christ who knows our pain. Therefore we can ask God for mercy, grace, help or forgiveness with complete confidence that he understands and is merciful.

We all fall short of the glory of God.
Romans 3:23

Lord, I am grateful for the following, thank you for...

Lord, I ask forgiveness for...

Lord, please guide me....

Dear God,

And when you
stand praying, if you
hold anything
against anyone,
forgive them, so that
your Father in
heaven may forgive
you your sins

Mark 11:25

REFLECTION

Whilst we expect God to forgive our sins and give us what we ask, we may not be as forgiving ourselves to others, getting into petty arguments and fallouts. Being in a Godly way means that we also need to put down our pride and forgive others and restore our relationships. Can you thing of anyone that you hold a grudge too and could follow God's example and forgive them? Could you also let them know this?

I can do all this through him who gives me strength
Philippians 4:13

Lord, I am grateful for the following, thank you for...

Lord, I ask forgiveness for...

Lord, please guide me....

Personal Prayer Section

Dear God,

And pray that we may be delivered from wicked and evil people, for not everyone has faith.

2 Thessalonians 3:2

REFLECTION

As we know, not everyone will act in a Godly way, not everyone has faith. Throughout our lives we will come across the paths of evil and wicked people. We can pray to God to be relieved of our burden of these people. Do you know such people? How do they make you feel?

For the Spirit God gave us does not make us timid, but gives us power,
love and self-discipline
2 Timothy 1:7

Lord, I am grateful for the following, thank you for...

Lord, I ask forgiveness for...

Lord, please guide me....

Personal Prayer Section

Dear God,

My soul is weary with sorrow; strengthen me according to your word.

Psalm 119:28

REFLECTION

Sometimes we can be so consumed with sadness that we feel our souls are exhausted and we cannot feel happiness ever again. There is always light at the end of the tunnel, always a new day, a new beginning and an ever open door of enlightenment to come our way. If you have sorrow of any degree, know that you are not alone, write about it now and seek strength from the Lord

What, then, shall we say in response to these things? If God is for us,
who can be against us
Romans 8:31

Lord, I am grateful for the following, thank you for...

Lord, I ask forgiveness for...

Lord, please guide me....

Personal Prayer Section

Dear God,

May God be
gracious to us and
bless us and make
his face shine on
us

Psalm 67:1

REFLECTION

When we turn our face to God and pray with a deep, faithful meaningful heart,
we will feel the grace of God shine back on us.
Not all prayers have to be of hardship, God loves the grateful and wants you so
much to be happy. Do you have grateful thoughts you could talk to God about
and show appreciation?

If they obey and serve him, they will spend the rest of their days in prosperity and their years in contentment.
Job 36:11

Lord, I am grateful for the following, thank you for...

Lord, I ask forgiveness for...

Lord, please guide me....

Personal Prayer Section

Dear God,

For a brief
moment I
abandoned you,
but with deep
compassion I will
bring you back

Isaiah 54:7

REFLECTION

We may feel that God has abandoned us at times, we may feel that it is impossible to find new faith or have trust again. We all have times of despair, but God will never leave you. Can you write about any times where you feel that you have been abandoned and how you have found solace?

Therefore go and make disciples of all nations, baptizing them in the name of the Father and of the Son and of the Holy Spirit, and teaching them to obey everything I have commanded you. And surely I am with you always, to the very end of the age

Matthew 28:19-20

Lord, I am grateful for the following, thank you for...

Lord, I ask forgiveness for...

Lord, please guide me....

Dear God,

Blessed is the one who perseveres under trial because, having stood the test, that person will receive the crown of life that the Lord has promised to those who love him

James 1:12

REFLECTION

For one who can keep faith at all times, through all of life's tribulations shall be rewarded with a richer experience here on earth and in heaven.
How does it make you feel to know that good can and will come to you? Do you feel as though you have what it takes to persevere? What are your dreams for yourself?

But blessed is the one who trusts in the LORD whose confidence is in him. They will be like a tree planted by the water that sends out its roots by the stream. It does not fear when heat comes; its leaves are always green. It has no worries in a year of drought and never fails to bear fruit.

Jeremiah 17:7-8

Lord, I am grateful for the following, thank you for...

Lord, I ask forgiveness for...

Lord, please guide me....

Personal Prayer Section

Dear God,

And forgive us our debts,
as we also have forgiven our
debtors.
And lead us not into temptation,
but deliver us from the evil one
For if you forgive other people
when they sin against you, your
heavenly Father will also forgive
you. But if you do not forgive
others their sins, your Father will
not forgive your sins

Matthew 6:12-15

REFLECTION

Applying ourselves in a Godly way means that we do onto others as we ask of ourselves. We regularly sin, it is human nature but we turn to God for forgiveness. To have true faith and allow God to work through us we most also forgive others. Forgiveness sets both parties free. Could you think back through your life at look at all of the vengeful thoughts that you have had and illness you may have wished on people? Can you find it in your heart to forgive them and yourself and move on to a much more peaceful state?

Jesus said, "Father, forgive them, for they do not know what they are doing. "And they divided up his clothes by casting lots
Luke 23:34

Lord, I am grateful for the following, thank you for...

Lord, I ask forgiveness for...

Lord, please guide me....

Personal Prayer Section

Dear God,

Be on your guard;
stand firm in the
faith;
be courageous;
be strong

Corinthians 16:13

REFLECTION

When you are acting in a Godly way towards yourself and others you can be confident in what you stand for. Don't let others stand in your way but peacefully be courageous and strong and stand up for what you know is the right way. Do you have times when you feel others attacking your beliefs, how do you deal with it?

But you are a chosen people, a royal priesthood, a holy nation, God's special possession, that you may declare the praises of him who called you out of darkness into his wonderful light.
1 Peter 2:9

Lord, I am grateful for the following, thank you for...

Lord, I ask forgiveness for...

Lord, please guide me….

Personal Prayer Section

Dear God,

He performs
wonders that cannot
be fathomed,
miracles that
cannot be counted

Job 5:9

REFLECTION

From the very first creation which was a miracle in itself, God creates miracles over and over again. The wonder of life is a blessed miracle in every way if you can see through child like eyes and a loving soul. Dislodging and removing any hardness or cynical view you have of the world will open up this ability to see miracles all around you, what a wonderful way to live, don't you agree?

He replied, "Because you have so little faith. Truly I tell you, if you have faith as small as a mustard seed, you can say to this mountain, 'Move from here to there,' and it will move. Nothing will be impossible for you.
Matthew 17:20

Lord, I am grateful for the following, thank you for...

Lord, I ask forgiveness for...

Lord, please guide me....

Personal Prayer Section

Dear God,

Nevertheless, I will bring health and healing to it; I will heal my people and will let them enjoy abundant peace and security

Jeremiah 33:6

REFLECTION

God can and does bring healing to all who have faith allowing them to enjoy abundant peace and security. Peace and security are everything that we need, being able to drop our shoulders, let down the defence and rest blissfully. I know that these things are what are most important to me now, but may not have been what I aspired to when I was much younger. What is important to you and have your dreams altered as you have gone through life?

For I know the plans I have for you, declares the LORD, plans to
prosper you and not to harm you, plans to give you hope and a future
Jeremiah 29:11

Lord, I am grateful for the following, thank you for...

Lord, I ask forgiveness for...

Lord, please guide me....

Personal Prayer Section

Dear God,

I sought
the LORD, and he
answered me;
he delivered me
from all my fears

Psalm 34:4

REFLECTION

He cannot help you if you don't look for him and find him, spilling your heart to him in the process. Often we all get caught up in life and realise that we have forgotten to turn our attention to him and pray.

Can you place a routine of prayer into your day? When was the last time you prayed?

Fear of man will prove to be a snare,
but whoever trusts in the LORD is kept safe
Proverbs 29:25

Lord, I am grateful for the following, thank you for...

Lord, I ask forgiveness for...

Lord, please guide me....

Personal Prayer Section

Dear God,

He will cover you with his feathers,
and under his wings you will find refuge;
his faithfulness will be your shield and rampart.
You will not fear the terror of night,
nor the arrow that flies by day

Psalm 91:4-5

REFLECTION

What a beautiful verse on God's love and protection! How could we ask of more than this from the Lord to feel his love and overcome our fears through the day and night?
Do you feel his protection and can you also offer protection and a safe place for others who need it?

The angel of the LORD encamps around those who fear him,
and he delivers them
Psalm 34:7

Lord, I am grateful for the following, thank you for...

Lord, I ask forgiveness for...

Lord, please guide me....

Personal Prayer Section

Dear God,

I thank my God
every time I
remember you.
In all my prayers
for all of you, I
always pray with
joy

Philippians 1:3-4

REFLECTION

Who can you thank the Lord for? Who has always been there for you,
has stood by you, has brought you joy, love and happiness.
Who are you thankful for?

You were taught, with regard to your former way of life, to put off your old self, which is being corrupted by its deceitful desires; to be made new in the attitude of your minds
Ephesians 4:2-3

Lord, I am grateful for the following, thank you for...

Lord, I ask forgiveness for...

Lord, please guide me....

Personal Prayer Section

Dear God,

The mouths of the
righteous utter
wisdom,
and their tongues
speak what is just.
The law of their God
is in their hearts;
their feet do not slip

Psalm 37:30-31

REFLECTION

Being part of God's love gives you a strength and steadfastness like no other.
The terminology of "their feet do not slip" can be adapted to, they do not give
into temptation or lose their faith regardless of circumstance.
This is a true sign of strength that will trickle down into every aspect of your life.
Do you feel you could attain this level of faith? It is open to all of us.

My dear brothers and sisters, take note of this: Everyone should be quick to listen, slow to speak and slow to become angry, because human anger does not produce the righteousness that God desires
James 1:19-20

Lord, I am grateful for the following, thank you for...

Lord, I ask forgiveness for...

Lord, please guide me....

_____

Personal Prayer Section

Dear God,

_____

For everyone who asks receives; the one who seeks finds; and to the one who knocks, the door will be opened

Matthew 7:8

REFLECTION

I am in love with this verse and have found it to be true in every aspect of my life. To receive what is in our hearts, we must ask, we must then look for the signs that this has been answered and then act on it. I.e.: the ask, the seek and the knock. We must do this with complete faith. What are you looking for right now in your life? Can you ask God for this and then be open for it to come to you? Are you aware that you must look for signs and act on them when they appear?

Now to him who is able to do immeasurably more than all we ask or imagine,
according to his power that is at work within us
Ephesians 3:20

Lord, I am grateful for the following, thank you for...

Lord, I ask forgiveness for...

Lord, please guide me....

Personal Prayer Section

Dear God,

Know that the Lord is God. It is he who made us, and we are his; we are his people, the sheep of his pasture

Psalm 100:3

REFLECTION

We belong to no man but God.
God is free and if we live in his way we shall be too.
Our bodies can be captive but our souls are always free when we have God. Are
you able to free your mind from your current surroundings and circumstances?

Give thanks to the **LORD**, for he is good; his love endures forever.
1 Chronicles 16:34

Lord, I am grateful for the following, thank you for...

Lord, I ask forgiveness for...

Lord, please guide me....

Personal Prayer Section

Dear God,

Whatever you do, work at it with all your heart, as working for the Lord, not for human masters

Colossians 3:23

REFLECTION

Working is a gift in which we can apply our own gifts and talents. Whatever we do and how we do it bears great weight on the outcome of our harvest. Working with God coming through us and for him will transform our work into joy and see us surpass our expectations of ourselves. Can you apply this attitude to your daily toil whatever it may be?

May the favor of the Lord our God rest on us; establish the work of our hands for us— yes, establish the work of our hands
Psalm 90:17

Lord, I am grateful for the following, thank you for...

Lord, I ask forgiveness for...

Lord, please guide me....

Personal Prayer Section

Dear God,

Your word is a
lamp for my feet,
a light on my path

Psalm 119:105

REFLECTION

What would you like to do, be or achieve in your life? Do you have thoughts like, "things like that never happen to me?" Or "I could never do that", "I'm not good/qualified enough?" If you believe in yourself as God believes in you and look for the flow of opportunity that God creates, you will find yourself, one step at a time working towards your dreams. What are they are where can you begin?

All hard work brings a profit, but mere talk leads only to poverty
Proverbs 14:23

Lord, I am grateful for the following, thank you for...

Lord, I ask forgiveness for...

Lord, please guide me....

Personal Prayer Section

Dear God,

Then God blessed the seventh day and made it holy, because on it he rested from all the work of creating that he had done.

Genesis 2:3

REFLECTION

When you have a dream in mind and you start working hard to create it, don't forget to reward yourself with a day of rest and holy reflection. Renewing your connection with God, thanking him for the opportunity, being grateful for all you have achieved and the doors that have opened to you. Then pray with a request of what you need for the following week to complete the next step and watch the majestic miracles that only God can do.

Anyone who does not provide for their relatives, and especially for their
own household, has denied the faith and is worse than an unbeliever
1 Timothy 5:8

Lord, I am grateful for the following, thank you for...

Lord, I ask forgiveness for...

Lord, please guide me....

Personal Prayer Section

Dear God,

And the priest said to them, "Go in peace. The journey on which you go is under the eye of the Lord.

Judges 18:6

REFLECTION

Starting a new journey from an aspect of peace is maybe a way that you haven't approached anything in your life before. Like most of us you may have approached all new ventures with a forcefulness and negative attitude of having to work against others as though we are all competing. I know I have been guilty of this. But there is another way. Start a new venture with an open heart, a peaceful one and think only of the task at hand and not what others are doing. Do you feel that this would be a new way of working for you?

Never be lazy, but work hard and serve the Lord
enthusiastically. Rejoice in our confident hope. Be patient in trouble,
and keep on praying.
Romans 12:11-12

Lord, I am grateful for the following, thank you for...

Lord, I ask forgiveness for...

Lord, please guide me....

Personal Prayer Section

Dear God,

You were taught, with regard
to your former way of life, to
put off your old self, which is
being corrupted by its deceitful
desires;
to be made new in the attitude
of your minds;
and to put on the new self,
created to be like God in true
righteousness and holiness.

Ephesians 4:22-24

REFLECTION

You've got this!! Look how far you have come in this last year, shedding the old ways and flowing from an aspect of righteousness and holiness.
Continue on your journey and may the Lord God truly bless you.
Can you reflect below on how your faith has strengthened and changed your life in the last year?

For everyone born of God overcomes the world
1;John 5:4

Lord, I am grateful for the following, thank you for...

Lord, I ask forgiveness for...

Lord, please guide me....

Personal Prayer Section

Dear God,

About the Author

Amaline is a poet, story teller and Prayer Journal creator with a strong compassion for people and a deep love of God. She had her first poem published at the age of 9 and has loved writing ever since, although only publishing her Journals and books in the last year.

She would love to hear how this Journal has helped you on your walk with God.

amalinecannings@outlook.com

Made in the USA
Columbia, SC
18 October 2024

44527633R00117